Original title:
The Abyss Beneath the Surface

Copyright © 2025 Creative Arts Management OÜ
All rights reserved.

Author: Alec Davenport
ISBN HARDBACK: 978-3-69081-475-1
ISBN PAPERBACK: 978-3-69081-971-8

Hidden Currents of Emotion

Beneath my smile, a whirlpool swirls,
Where socks and secrets lose their pearls.
I laugh while dodging submerged fears,
   With laughter masking all my tears.

Banana peels float, a jester's joke,
With hidden depths that sometimes poke.
When life gets weird, I just might mime,
   To keep afloat through riddles sublime.

The Unseen Dangers of Still Waters

A mirror lake, so sleek and calm,
Yet fish wear suits, and they mean harm.
With every ripple, mischief stirs,
As water lilies crack dry slurs.

The ducks exchange a knowing glance,
Plotting a waddle, this is their dance.
Still waters hide their loudest screams,
As frogs launch into wild, wild dreams.

Threads of Tension Beneath Calm Seas

In tranquil blues, a drama plays,
Where crabs debate in crustacean ways.
A shark and goldfish share a wink,
While octopuses plot over a drink.

Silken strands of laughter rise,
As jellyfish twirl in disguise.
With bubbles bursting, tales unfold,
Of tidal pranks and treasures bold.

Voices of Silenced Depths

In quiet depths, a clam begins to sing,
While seaweed dancers groove like spring.
With conch shells blaring, howls arise,
Unheard by sailors, oh what a surprise!

With muffled jokes from coral friends,
And fish who giggle as the sea bends.
Their laughter ripples through the brine,
Where deep-sea secrets twist entwine.

The Dark Canvas of Dreams

In dreams we race on jellybean trains,
While fish wear hats and sing bizarre refrains.
A cat in a tux, sipping fine green tea,
Whispers secrets to a dancing bumblebee.

To dive through skies painted with absurdity,
Where puddles reflect our wildest curiosity.
A world on the edge, where logic takes flight,
And time does the cha-cha under disco light.

Veiled Depths of the Soul

Beneath our skin lies a carnival ride,
With clowns that laugh and a goat that slides.
A treasure trove of misplaced socks,
And ice cream mountains that weathered the clocks.

When we dive too deep for our own good sense,
We find polka-dotted mermaids, oh so dense.
They trade you a joke for a slice of pie,
As the bubbles of laughter just sail on by.

Secrets Swirling in the Dark Water

In waters so murky, where fishes can't swim,
A wise turtle croons a quirky little hymn.
With octopi drawing on bubbles galore,
And seahorses arguing on the ocean floor.

What mysteries lurk in the seaweed so thick?
Perhaps it's a drama with a very old trick.
As crabs hold auditions for the next big show,
While plankton all cheer, 'We want more glow!'

Silence of the Sunken Worlds

Beneath the surface, where giggles reside,
Lives a fish who thinks he's a captain with pride.
He sails on a cork with a grin ear to ear,
While sea cucumbers cheer, 'It's party time, dear!'

But wait, what's that lurking, so sly and so shy?
An octopus whispering, 'Oh my, oh my!'
He spins a tall tale of swimming too fast,
In a world full of giggles, a dive unsurpassed.

Depths of Unseen Shadows

In the dark, where socks go missing,
A monster laughs, forever kissing.
With each flap of a fin, I fear,
It's just a dog, or is it a deer?

The plumbed pits where crumbs are lost,
They swim and dance, at what cost?
The jellybeans plot their sweet revenge,
For all the times we've failed to binge.

Whispers in the Deep

Bubbles rise with gossip tall,
Did you hear that? The cat might fall!
Sneaky whispers float around,
Is it the fish? Or just our sound?

Mermaids giggle, as they glide,
Winking at sailors, trying to hide.
But ever so sly, they share their tales,
Of questionable style and seaweed nails.

Chasms of Unspoken Fears

In shadowed depths, I feel a chill,
Is it phobia or maybe a thrill?
Giant squids that text at night,
Telling jokes about their flight.

Unexpected frights that make me scream,
Like soggy bread, a doughy dream.
But what's lurking just out of sight?
Maybe just a fish with a frightful bite?

Echoes from the Ocean Floor

Down below, the seaweed sways,
With cryptic messages, in fishy ways.
They play charades, oh what a sight,
   While I just ponder if I'm right.

Crabs click-clack, a symphony,
Do they argue or sing in glee?
With each echo, a new prank awaits,
Like tucking in shells for dinner dates!

Currents of the Subconscious

In the depths where thoughts do swim,
A goldfish dreams of life on a whim.
With bubbles popping, laughter flows,
As seaweed dances and a snail throws bows.

The crabs hold court, a shellfish rave,
While jellyfish glide, oh so brave!
Each wave a joke, a splash of glee,
With octopi playing hide and seek, whee!

The Weight of Sunken Thoughts

A rock sinks slowly, a ponderous feat,
While fish swim by like, "Is this a treat?"
The anchor's grumpy, it's always down,
Wishing for wings to fly, not drown.

A tuba sounds from the depths unseen,
As laughter echoes in bubbles of green.
The weight of musings, heavy yet bright,
Like an otter juggling in moonlight.

Dreamscapes of the Deep

In dreamscapes where the seaweed sighs,
Mermaids giggle and fish wear ties.
The starfish throw a dealer's hand,
While clowns in snorkels lend an odd band.

A whale hums tunes that tickle the tide,
With crustaceans dancing, full of pride.
A seahorse sings baritone so deep,
As turtles yawn, and the dolphins leap.

Monsters in the Silence

In shadows lurk the fears that beam,
Like the Kraken's grin, a comical dream.
With wiggly tentacles, it gives a wink,
While flounders gossip and dolphins think.

The silence bursts with a punchline snort,
As eels play tag on a seaweed court.
Even the deep can tickle you funny,
Where sea monsters lurk, oh so sunny!

Phantoms of the Submerged Realm

Bubbles dance and giggle, what a sight,
Mermaids pirouette, in moonlit delight.
Octopuses juggle with ease, such flair,
Even seaweed joins in, swaying with care.

Sea turtles crack jokes, all in good fun,
While starfish throw parties, beneath the sun.
Fish wear bowties, it's quite the affair,
As jellyfish glow, they float without a care.

Unraveled in Midnight's Grasp

In shadows where eels spin tales so sly,
Crabs in tuxedos complain, oh my!
Barnacles gossip, they cling and they chat,
While surfboards wait, sharing tales of a cat.

A whale sings lullabies in a laughable tone,
Fish laugh in bubbles, for skills they have grown.
In this midnight dance, all creatures unite,
As fishes tell stories, funny and light.

The Hidden Pulse of Silence

Under a curtain of silence, cracks a smile,
Clowns of the ocean, they're never in style.
Pufferfish puffing, hilariously round,
While dolphins play tricks, in laughter they're found.

Seahorses debating, their tails all in knots,
Seashells whisper secrets about seagull thoughts.
The wit of the waves, oh, such cheeky grace,
In this quiet ruckus, they find their place.

Depths of Undiscovered Whispers

In hidden depths, where jokes are profound,
Anglerfish flickering lights all around.
Gremlins of depth, with a twist and a turn,
Share pranks with the crabs; oh, how we learn!

Tangled in laughter, sea cucumbers sway,
Blabbermouth fish share tales of the day.
Anemones giggle, their humor unstopped,
And everyone stifles when a clownfish plopped!

Beneath the Calm

In placid waters, fish all grin,
But wait! A shoe just tumbled in!
With bubbles rising, laughter flows,
Are shoes now fish? Who really knows?

The ducks parade with quite the flair,
While frogs debate who'll jump the air.
A crab in shades thinks it's a star,
"Oh, look at me! I'm gonna go far!"

Turmoil Stirs

Beneath the surface, things get wild,
A duckling's tantrum, oh so riled.
A whirlpool forms of bits and bobs,
"Hey, who threw my lunch? Robbing mobs!"

The turtles grumble, fish just roll,
In a swirl of chaos, they lose control.
A guppy giggles, "Is this a show?"
"Can I have front row? I'm the star of the flow!"

Laments of the Leaking Tide

As water seeps from holes unknown,
Sea creatures sigh, "We're not alone!"
A jellyfish lost a bit of flair,
"Hey, I prefer a proper chair!"

Seashells chatter, gossiping low,
Who's next to wash ashore, who knows?
The beach's a stage, the waves on cue,
"Next!" cries a crab, "More drama, woohoo!"

Undercurrents of Dread

The fish are plotting, whispers swell,
"We'll start a band and sing quite well!"
But wait—who's leading? A starfish chimes,
"Just follow my lead and forget the rhymes!"

A distant rumble stirs the sand,
"Does this mean we're starting a band?"
But then it's chaos, fins all collide,
"Hey! Keep your scales on your side!"

Echoes in Tranquil Waters

Splashing echoes, laughter swells,
As fish play tag in underwater bells.
A pufferfish breaks out in cheer,
"Bubbles away! We're free this year!"

A starry night, the sea shines bright,
Fish sing songs, under soft moonlight.
"Join our chorus, come share this fun!"
"For soon the tide rolls in, we can't outrun!"

Beneath the Softening Gaze

In a world where fish wear ties,
And dolphins fool with clever lies,
A shrimp debates life's big demands,
While octopuses clap with their hands.

The seaweed waltzes with flair so bright,
While crabs throw shade, what a delight!
Anemones primp in morning light,
As starfish hold beauty contests at night.

Midnight's Burden Beneath

The catfish grumbles, 'Where's my snack?'
With all this garbage on my back!
A puffer's feeling quite the funk,
While eels get tangled in the junk.

The hermit crab's on home decor,
Swapping shells during a sea-floor tour,
Clownfish attempt a stand-up set,
Only to drown in a sea of regret.

The Secrets Held by Silent Waves

Whispers ride on frothy tides,
As jellyfish play marinas' guides,
A walrus laughs at sunken ships,
While barnacles cheer with little quips.

Seahorses gossip, secrets in tow,
About the currents and tides they know,
Fish in tuxedos swim past the reef,
Saying, 'Let's dance, it's beyond belief!'

When Stillness is a Lament

The sea is calm, too calm for fun,
A lobster's grumpy, 'I'm not done!'
The crabs compete in a dance-off whirl,
While sea cucumbers just twirl and furl.

An octopus sighs, 'Is this the life?'
With tentacles tangled in existential strife,
But then a clownfish makes a quip,
Turning the mood on a joyful flip.

Chasms of the Unseen

In shadows, I spill my soda,
A phantom slip, what a curd!
The cat laughs, it's quite a show,
Just a clumsy dance, absurd.

Underneath my wobbly chair,
Lies my snack, it thinks it's sly.
Popcorn smiles, a crunchy air,
I swear it winked, oh my, oh my!

Beneath the floor, a sock brigade,
They plot to steal my favorite shoes.
I swear they're in a secret trade,
With crumpled notes, they share the blues.

Yet in this space, such laughter swells,
Echoes from the depths untold.
For even in these hidden wells,
Jokes can thrive, and joy unfold.

Lurking in the Void

An empty fridge, what a delight,
It whispers tales of yesteryear.
Lost veggies in their quiet fight,
Pasta noodles shed a tear.

Behind my couch, a world so bold,
Dust bunnies sprout with flair and glee.
They throw a dance party in the cold,
Who knew they'd welcome me for tea?

In corners dark, my shoes conspire,
To tango when I'm not around.
Each squeak and slide, they never tire,
In this unseen fest, joy is found.

Oh, lurking void, you're never still,
A comedy of hidden fate.
With every creak, you tease and thrill,
In your depths, we laugh, we wait.

Depths of Hidden Sorrows

Oh, the laundry pile—a mountain high,
It hides my dignity, I fear.
That lost sock's tale, it makes me sigh,
It fled to realms of fun, I hear.

While weeds conspire beneath the stone,
Their laughter bubbles 'neath my feet.
A garden host, I sit alone,
Yet plot my schemes for veggie defeat.

Lost in the back of my drawer's plea,
Old receipts throw a party, bold.
They chirp of times when I felt free,
And steal my change—their jokes retold.

Underneath my layers, life digests,
With humor bright, despite its strife.
In hidden depths, I, too, attest,
Laughter rules this crazy life.

When Darkness Breathes

A shadow stretched across my bed,
A whisper asked for midnight snacks.
The fridge replied, 'You've got the bread, '
While teasing me with missed attacks.

Out in the yard, the crickets croon,
As night drapes softly on the ground.
They serenade the moon's round tune,
In croaks and hops, the joy is found.

My closet holds a secret stash,
Of costumes from a different time.
A pirate's hat, a comical clash,
They flourish wild, stripped of their grime.

When darkness breathes, our giggles rise,
A choir hidden from the dawn.
In every shadow, jest supplies,
To keep us laughing until morn.

The Current of Forgotten Echoes

Beneath the waves, a sock swims free,
Its lone adventure, oh woe is me!
Lost in the depths, it floats with grace,
While fish all giggle, 'What a funny place!'

A jellyfish glows, a disco ball,
While crabby critters hold a grand sprawl.
They groove and dance in underwater glee,
Mocking their neighbors, a sight to see!

A clam shouts loud, 'I'm royalty here!'
While octopuses hide from a murky smear.
With all this fun, who needs a shore?
The ocean's a party, let's dance some more!

But as they twirl and celebrate bold,
A sea turtle sighs, 'I'm getting old.'
As bubbles rise up, they float with cheer,
In this deep, dark world filled with laughter and fear!

Murmurs from the Netherworld

In a boggy realm where whispers play,
The frogs debate what to have today.
'Grasshoppers sautéed or flies with rice?'
They croak and squawk; it's not so nice!

An alligator teases his best friend,
'You'll never guess where this tale will end!'
With scales that shimmer and a grin so wide,
He jokes about the fish that try to hide.

A ghostly eel glides with whimsy and flair,
Dancing through weeds, he's lost in his hair.
'Careful below, there's a hook in the deep!'
He cackles and bubbles, causing a heap!

So listen closely, to what they say,
For the Netherworld is a comical play.
Where the fish tell tales of their luck and charm,
And everyone swims in delightful alarm!

Where Shadows Skim the Surface

Under the moon, the fish play hide,
While shadows waltz on the water's glide.
'Is that a shark or just my mate?'
They laugh and giggle at their own fate.

With a splash and a flick, the catfish dart,
Telling tall tales that make them smart.
A turtle quips, 'I'm slow but wise!'
As his friends race past, 'Just look at those guys!'

The whispers rise from the pond so wide,
With tales of frogs that jump with pride.
They claim to be champions of the croak,
While a dragonfly zooms in for a joke.

In this shadowy realm, the laughter's loud,
With bubbles and splashes, the fish feel proud.
They dance and they frolic; they never tire,
In the depths of the night, their hearts are on fire!

Ripples of Hidden Fears

Beneath the lily pads, a frog frets alone,
For today he forgot how to groan.
With awkward hops and a ribbit gone bad,
His buddies all chuckle; they're not even mad.

A fish swims by, sporting a frown,
'What's with the hops? You're the talk of the town!'
But froggy just sighs, 'It's a tough kind of day!'
As ripples emerge and dance far away.

Turtles take bets on how far he'll glide,
While crickets compete with their song and pride.
His quirky hops earn a round of applause,
In his heart he wonders, 'What's keeping me paused?'

The fears wash away as laughter takes hold,
With each silly misstep, their friendship grows bold.
In the hidden waters, where secrets reside,
The fun never ceases, and joy's the best guide!

The Uncharted Depths of Sorrow

In a sea of mismatched socks,
I sink, but still, I mock.
Lost in the depths of my laundry,
A treasure map is just a conundrum.

Waves of crumbs beneath my feet,
A snack attack—a tasty feat.
Pirate ships of half-eaten cakes,
Charting routes through kitchen lakes.

With every plunder, I gain a frown,
Finding joy in my crumbly crown.
Where's the gold? Just flaky crumbs,
As my stomach silently drums.

A shipwreck on spilled coffee tides,
Lost in the realm where caffeine hides.
No groans of sorrow, just silly laughs,
As I paddle through life's caffeine gaffs.

Layers of Silent Turmoil

Beneath my bed lies a beast,
An ogre made of dust and feasts.
He grumbles soft, yet eats my shoes,
A strange companion with odd views.

Layers of papers, a fortress grown,
A kingdom where my emails moan.
Each scroll a soldier, lost in time,
Yet I see gags in every rhyme.

My social life, a tangled vine,
In its knots, I often whine.
But in my heart, a giggle grows,
As I stumble through life's silly shows.

Like a turtle without a shell,
I waddle around, oh so well.
For as I dive into this mess,
I find laughter in the stress.

Dark Waters of Solitude

In puddled thoughts where fish don't swim,
I chat with shadows on a whim.
They nod politely, but don't reply,
As I ponder why my cat can't fly.

Jellyfish of doubt float by,
Windowless rooms make me sigh.
Yet in the silence, I find a tune,
Dancing alone, under the moon.

Octopus arms reach out for snacks,
As I swim back from daily cracks.
In my clam shell of quirky dreams,
I chase the laughter past the screams.

With every ripple that I send,
Solitude's my awkward friend.
We share a joke, we laugh it through,
In fishy waters, just me and you.

The Quiet Struggle Below

In the depths of my fridge, a tale unfolds,
A yogurt cup that just won't mold.
It whispers secrets in a chill,
While I'm left to wonder, eat or kill?

The ice packs grumble, the veggies pout,
Who knew a drawer could cause such doubt?
Pickle jars hold laughter deep inside,
In this cool abyss, no need to hide.

Beneath the surface of my snacks,
A party blooms—hidden prattacks.
Where fries and pies form a merry team,
Life turns comical, like a crazy dream.

As I raid the depths for hidden treats,
My heart hums soft, with silly beats.
For in this struggle, oh so profound,
Laughter echoes where joy is found.

Tides of Hidden Despair

The ocean laughs with bubbles bright,
While fish wear frowns, what a sight!
A crab is lost, he lacks a map,
And seagulls plan their lunchtime nap.

The tides are high, a perfect tease,
While barnacles plot 'which boat to freeze?'
A dolphin jokes, swishing about,
'Watch out! Here comes a hungry trout!'

As seaweed dances with a sway,
It giggles softly, come what may.
A jellyfish floats, lost in glee,
While sailors argue tea or pee.

The waves crash in with cheeky flair,
Each splashing sound a grand affair.
Yet deep below, a funny sight,
The octopus tangled in his flight.

Beneath the Veil of Stillness

In calm blue depths where squids belt tunes,
With beatboxing beats that make you swoon.
A clam exhibits shyness great,
While mermaids giggle over fate.

The coral reefs are bustling towns,
Where grouper gossip all around.
A turtle slips — oh, what a clatter!
And fish argue just what's the matter.

The seaweed whispers secrets deep,
Of how it dreams of mountain steep.
A starfish plays a one-legged dance,
While crabs roll dice for their next chance.

Beneath the stillness, oh so sly,
The fish all plot to get high and dry.
With bubbles popping, mischief thrives,
It's just another day in sea lives.

Secrets in the Briny Dark

There's laughter trapped in jars of brine,
As sea cucumbers sip on wine.
A dolphin's jest has them in fits,
While eels throw shade, calling out hits.

The currents twist, what a sly game,
A shrimp declares he's found a fame!
A crab, confused, mistakes a sock,
Decides instead to take a walk.

The anglerfish grins, quite the show,
"Come closer, friend, do you not know?
I'm hosting parties, fish invite,
But please don't bring that feisty bite!"

In shadows deep, the laughter swells,
With ticklish tides and silly spells.
How strange it is, so wild and stark,
The underwater truths of the dark.

Currents of Forgotten Dreams

As tides roll through with dreams anew,
Some fish just ponder what to chew.
A blowfish takes a selfie right,
While parrotfish squawk, "Take it light!"

The ocean floors hold tales untold,
Of sea stars clashing, fierce and bold.
A snail in shells, all wrapped in style,
Claims he's the king — but that's denial!

The currents sway in zigzag lines,
And squid stick out their goofball signs.
They giggle loud, as bubbles pop,
Oh, what a wild underwater hop!

In liquid realms where laughter blooms,
The sea sings of its joys and dooms.
A world beneath where dreams still gleam,
The ocean's heart, a funny theme.

Echoes from Beneath Calm Faces

Beneath the smiles, a giggle hides,
A pocket of secrets, where nonsense resides.
Cheshire grins keep the laughter near,
While serious faces hide the cheer.

A wave of silence swallows the room,
Yet chocolate thoughts begin to bloom.
Tickles of snickers echo and ripple,
As humor bubbles beneath each scribble.

With a wink and a nod, we play our game,
Pretending it's normal but we're all the same.
The calmest of looks betray what's inside,
Where mirth and mayhem so slyly glide.

So raise your glass to the unseen levity,
For what's calm on top is pure festivity.
In the depths, a party waits with glee,
Let's toast to the laughs that aren't meant to be!

Sinking into Solitude

In the bath of solitude, bubbles gleam,
But in my mind, I spin quite the dream.
Rubber ducks float as my thoughts twist,
Who knew being alone could feel like bliss?

I sink deeper down, just me and my soap,
Lost in the layers of thoughts and hope.
Shampoo rivers flow as I ponder and giggle,
Where thoughts get tangled and feelings wiggle.

Loofah in hand, I scrub away doubt,
While visions of sugarplums dance all about.
Laughter erupts like waves without shame,
Finding joy in solitude isn't quite lame.

So here's to our soppy, solo sprees,
Where we find humor in quiet seas.
Sinking down deep, but laughing all night,
With ducky friends who make everything right!

The Veil of What Lurks Below

Under the surface, the silliness stirs,
A dance of delight that tickles and purrs.
The shadows may linger, but oh, what a sight,
In the depths, there's a party of sheer delight!

A curtain of laughter drapes over our woes,
We peek underneath for the giggle that grows.
With shadows of grins and whispers of glee,
The things that we hide aren't scary, you see.

With every step down, the silliness swells,
Where hiccups of humor launch jubilant spells.
The veil parts to share what we keep out of sight,
Releasing the chuckles that dance in the night.

So lift up the curtain, let's give it a whirl,
In the depths of our fears, let the laughter unfurl.
We'll wave to the shadows that haunt our release,
In a sea of hilarity, we find our peace!

Caverns of the Mind

In caverns of thought, where nonsense can roam,
Thoughts bounce like balls in an echoing dome.
A treasure of giggles swims deep in the caves,
Where whispers of silliness flow like warm waves.

Monsters of logic, all dressed in black ties,
Hide under rocks and roll quaint little eyes.
But with a quick quip or the lightest of jests,
We turn their frowns into mirthful quests!

With lanterns of laughter lighting each bend,
The paths of absurdity never seem to end.
Each turn reveals joy, absurd as it seems,
In caverns of whimsy, we chase after dreams.

So journey with me through the twists and the turns,
Where the fires of humor flicker and burn.
Together we'll conquer the vast, silly plight,
In the caverns of our minds, we'll dance until night!

Murmurs from the Depths

Whispers float from depths unknown,
A fish in pants, all on his own.
He lost his hat, it swam away,
Now he's the fashion of the bay.

Crabs dance by with shells so bright,
Wearing shades, they think it's right.
Jellyfish play on stilts of gold,
Trying to strut, but they look bold.

A seaweed band strikes up a tune,
The octopus seems out of tune.
With every pluck, a laugh resounds,
When bass gives beats, the crowd confounds.

A dolphin tells a knock-knock joke,
He opens wide to woo a bloke.
But with a splash, all joy is doused,
When laughter sinks, the fish are doused.

Constellations Beneath the Waves

Down below, the starlight twinkles,
A starfish winks, while seaweed crinkles.
The moonlight gives a jelly glow,
But fish seem lost in cosmic flow.

A whale swims by, he seems bemused,
While seahorses wear ties, confused.
With bubbles caught in swirling dance,
They trip on currents, lost in trance.

Crab astronauts on quests of whim,
Pursuing dreams both sly and dim.
A tiny ship of coral wood,
Navigates waves as best it could.

With laughter echoing 'round the reef,
The creatures find their comic relief.
In cosmic depths, they rise and sink,
Forming friendships in the ocean's blink.

Navigating the Depths of the Mind

In thoughts where fish and thoughts collide,
A clownfish wears a silly stride.
Navigating mazes made of thought,
Trying to find what it has sought.

An anglerfish, with glowing bait,
Goes fishing for the latest date.
But what a catch, a confused stare,
When squids say, 'No, we don't care!'

Each day brings underwater dreams,
Where bubbles pop and laughter beams.
The starfish guides our silly quest,
With wisdom from the ocean's jest.

Inside the mind, where chaos reigns,
We find delight, but also pains.
Yet bubbles burst with laughter's might,
In the depths where thoughts take flight.

Shattered Reflections in the Water

Reflections swirl in waters clear,
A fish peeks in, then shows a cheer.
With silly faces, they play tricks,
The mirror laughs, it's all a mix.

A tangled net of mirrored glee,
Where clowns of the sea run wild and free.
They strike a pose, then boom, they splash,
With every giggle, the ripples crash.

In broken light, a kraken grins,
With jester's cap, he boldly spins.
Trying to catch his own deft gaze,
In rippling waves, where madness plays.

But laughter stirs the tranquil scenes,
As playful jests exit like dreams.
Though images crack, the joy stays bright,
In shattered views, we find delight.

Harboring Shadows of Past

In the closet lurks my ex,
Frog-shaped hat and socks perplex.
Ghostly dances in the gloom,
Who invites this artsy doom?

Dust bunnies waltz in silly haste,
Chasing crumbs, oh, what a waste!
Whispers of a cat's debate,
"Is it dinner time or fate?"

Old regrets on shelves do sit,
Wearing frowns, they never quit.
But laughter cracks the shadows wide,
As I chuckle, here's my guide!

So let it all float to the sea,
Past blunders filled with glee,
For in these memories I find,
A funny heart, a grateful mind.

The Weight of Drowned Thoughts

Bubbles rise from thoughts submerged,
Like fish that sing, a bit diverged.
What a thought! A tuba plays,
While pondering the laundry maze.

Soggy socks, they float around,
Like swimmers lost, in dreams they drown.
Ideas drift in, oh so vague,
Chasing ducks that dance and beg.

Weights of worries, leaden ties,
Yet laughter shines in unforeseen eyes.
Why take life too seriously,
When giggles float so effortlessly?

So here's to thoughts that sink and swim,
As laughter bubbles, smiles begin.
Lighten up, let your spirit sway,
Drowned thoughts can surf another day!

Beneath the Surface

Monsters bask in shallow pools,
Wearing shades, they skip the rules.
Bubble baths for silly fish,
They'd change the world if only swished.

Crabs in tuxedos dance around,
At the ball where laughter's found.
Eel in stripes, a sight to see,
Flipping through the comic spree.

Turtles hold a stand-up show,
With punchlines that will ebb and flow.
"Why did the fish cross the stream?"
To boogie with the seaweed team!

So let's dive deep, and take a peek,
In this giggly world, there's no critique.
Beneath the waves where fun resides,
We'll paddle where silly smiles glide.

Stillness Brews

Calm waters hide a bubbling plot,
Stillness brews, then beans are hot!
Coffee cups swim, drift along,
To the rhythm of a quirky song.

Fish in hats discuss the wine,
While ducks share tales of beachy time.
Under the quiet, a conga line,
Livin' it up, feeling just fine!

When stillness reigns, what a delight,
Jellyfish twirl, holding on tight.
They whisper jokes 'midst seaweed fronds,
Tickling tides with silly ponds.

Oh, the laughter brewed so near,
Even the rocks can't help but cheer!
In tranquil depths where giggles dwell,
Life's a party, oh, isn't it swell?

In the Depths of the Mind's Eye

Peering down where thoughts collide,
A lightbulb twinkles, oh, what a ride!
Ideas swim like dolphins free,
Making waves of joy and glee.

Stirring dreams in a fishy stew,
Carrots add a playful hue.
"Why did the ghost wear a dress?"
To manifest its silkiness!

Floating by, a whale with flair,
Winks at doubts, gives all a scare.
Fancy thoughts do pirouette,
Chasing fears, no need to fret!

In this sea where giggles float,
Riding currents, a silly boat.
With each splash, the laughter grows,
In the depths, joy overflows!

Trails of the Unremembered

Forgotten paths where shadows play,
And squirrels dance the night away.
Old socks lurk behind the trees,
Searching for their partners with ease.

Maps drawn in chalk, all washed away,
They lead to places we can't say.
The dog has claimed the secrets here,
While I just scratch my head in cheer.

The owls hoot tunes from long ago,
While I attempt my stand-up show.
Each giggle echoes in the night,
As clouds roll in to join the fight.

So here I wander, a fool in jest,
With mismatched shoes, I feel my best.
Life's a puzzle, a quirky game,
While trails of laughter stay the same.

Submerged Landscapes of Memory

Beneath the waves of thought and time,
Swim fish that whisper in odd rhyme.
There's a turtle wearing a silly hat,
And jellyfish who host a tea party chat.

Old groceries float, a surreal sight,
Bananas doing the moonwalk right.
A shopping list drifts in the foam,
It sings of snacks from long ago home.

Sandcastles rise, but quickly fall,
Memory's tides come to enthrall.
Shells of laughter wash ashore,
Each one tells tales of yore.

Dive in deep, don't lose your grin,
For laughter bubbles where it's been.
Flip-flops splash in a joyous flood,
As we wade through life's silly mud.

The Trench of Longing

In a trench where wishes grow,
I find my dreams, but where's the show?
A fish in a bowtie makes a stand,
While popcorn rains like grains of sand.

Desires drift like paper boats,
That capsize quick in silly floats.
With giggles echoing in the night,
I chase my thoughts with sheer delight.

Banana peels dance on the brink,
As I ponder life and what I think.
Oh, how the shadows love a tale,
Of kittens wearing flowers as a veil.

Here in the trench, I find my cheer,
While old yearnings tap at my ear.
A toast to wishes, come what may,
In this trench, let laughter stay.

Enveloped in the Mysterious Dusk

As dusk wraps round like a cozy quilt,
Even the stars seem oddly built.
A raccoon juggles apples with flair,
While shadows dance without a care.

In the gentle dark, a wise old frog,
Hops through secrets in a fog.
His croaks are jokes from times gone by,
Making the crickets giggle and sigh.

Cakes float by like dreams deferred,
While nightingale sings the most absurd.
The moon can't stop its bright ballet,
As trees sway gently in their play.

Here in the dusk, life's quirks abound,
With laughter rising from the ground.
Enveloped in joy, we must agree,
The mysteries stay, but we're still free.

The Quietude of Lost Thoughts

In the corners of my mind, they play,
Lost thoughts dancing, gone astray.
Like socks in the dryer, they spin about,
Whispering secrets that I can't tout.

They giggle at me, just out of reach,
Mumbling wisdom they'd like to teach.
If only I could catch their parade,
I'd write a best-seller, make a grand trade.

Yet here I sit, a cluttered mess,
With puns and riddles, I must confess.
The lost thoughts party hard, it's clear,
While I'm stuck here, sipping my beer.

Oh, the quietude, a crafty beast,
Fooling me daily, a hilarious feast.
If only they'd leave me a note or two,
But they opted for fun, instead to pursue.

Underneath the Shimmering Lies

Underneath the glint and glow,
Foolish fables start to grow.
Shimmering tales with sparkly flair,
Are they truths or just in the air?

A unicorn pranced in my coffee cup,
While talking fish invite me to sup.
Every glittery story, oh so bright,
Turns into a chuckle at midnight's height.

With every tale that twists and bends,
Reality wiggles, and laughter extends.
I sip on my soda, a grin on my face,
For the whoppers we tell, it's a wild race!

So here's to the sparkles that lead us astray,
The laughs and the giggles that come out to play.
Underneath the glimmers, embrace the jest,
For life's little lies are simply the best!

The Silence of Forgotten Battles

In the quiet of yesterday's brawl,
I trip over memories, each one a ball.
Sock puppets failing on grand battlefields,
While I'm just stuck with my rubbery shields.

The war of the snacks, oh what a fright!
Cookies and chips clashing by night.
I hear them rumble, a faint crinkle sound,
As crumbs of defeat scatter all around.

Victory smells like pizza and pie,
But I tend to nap when the stakes are high.
Forgotten battles make me chuckle and snort,
As I wade through the wreckage of last week's sport.

So here's to my fumbles, loud and unplanned,
In the silence of chaos, I joyfully stand.
For every hilariously lost little fight,
Leaves me with giggles to ponder at night.

Lurking Afterglow

From shadows, laughter starts to rise,
With mischievous chuckles and twinkling eyes.
An afterglow lingers, teasing my mind,
A jester's delight, oh how it's designed!

I chase it around, like a kitten at play,
Pouncing on jokes that slip away.
Each giggle a wink, a sly little nudge,
In this delightful farce, I refuse to budge.

The glow leads me on, with whimsy so bright,
Through corridors strange in the dead of night.
Where ticklish shadows play tag on my feet,
And laughter erupts with each silly tweet.

So here's to the antics that dance in the dark,
To the gleaming whims that spark every lark.
In the lurking afterglow, joy shall abide,
With laughter as my ever-joyous guide.

Where Surface and Depth Collide

In the pond where frogs all croak,
A fish floats by, it starts to joke.
"Why did the turtle cross the shore?"
To see if he could swim some more!

Bubbles rise, a secret spree,
"Dive down, my friend, come swim with me!"
A splash, a laugh, the minnows dance,
In this wet world, we all take a chance!

The water's cool, the laughter calls,
A diving beetle, he takes his falls.
"Careful now, don't drink the stream!"
Or you'll wake up from your sleep dream!

Fishy tales in twilight gleam,
Where jokes float up, a lighthearted beam.
Under the waves, the giggles abide,
In this goofy place where depths coincide!

The Dark Heart of Still Waters

In the still of night, a splash now rings,
A worried frog now flaps his wings.
"What's lurking down in shadowy depths?"
Just my old shoes, with lots of missteps!

A shadow glides, it brushes near,
"Oh dear! Another angler's gear!"
"Why do they fish if the catch can't chat?"
"Perhaps for the thrill, or just for a hat!"

A catfish winks from under the dock,
"Hey, landlubbers, it's all a big clock!"
Time swims round, in circles we go,
"Who knew the creek had a comedy show?"

Ripples laugh at the moon's soft song,
In this watery place, we all belong.
The dark may hide, but jesters emerge,
While fishy puns and giggles converge!

Hidden Harmonies Beneath the Waves

Under the currents, the secrets play,
With seaweed swaying in a funky way.
A clam snaps shut, it knows the tune,
To rock the reef by the light of the moon!

Octopus spots, with eight happy arms,
Doing the conga, with endless charms.
"Got rhythm?" they ask, a squid joins in,
Turning the tide with a cheeky grin.

The sea cucumbers hum a low beat,
While crabs dance sideways, quick on their feet.
"Dive down, friends, and join the fun!"
Where laughter flows, and beams like the sun!

Hidden treasures in laughter's embrace,
Under the waves, there's always a trace.
So come for a swim, and bring your tunes,
In these watery depths, we'll hear the boons!

Voices from the Inky Black

In shadows deep where fish may sing,
Bubbles dance and seahorses fling.
Crabs argue over who is best,
While seaweed teases the coral crest.

A whale sways to an underwater beat,
Finding rhythm in the silted street.
Octopus plays with a game of charades,
As turtles laugh in their leafy glades.

The jellyfish glow like disco lights,
Hosting parties for the bugs in flights.
Anemones sway like they know a dance,
While starfish gossip, giving a glance.

On a shell phone, a clam will call,
While a clownfish pranks, making others fall.
Beneath the waves, things are absurd,
Life's a comedy where silence is heard.

The Imagery of What Lies Below

In murky depths, the eels will giggle,
As sea cucumbers start to wiggle.
A fish in glasses reads the news,
While crabs wear hats and argue their views.

Seashell selfies are all the rage,
With lobsters striving to be on stage.
An octopus dons a polka dot tie,
As minnows swim by with an awkward sigh.

Beneath the waves, humor's a gem,
With shrimps that prank like a fickle friend.
Starfish wear shades, looking quite cool,
While the sea urchins skip class at the school.

A sulking ray just lost a bet,
To a fish who collects all the debt.
In this realm where nonsense rules,
Everything's fun, even schools of fools.

Fragments of Forgotten Dreams

A squid writes poems on a sea floor slate,
While fish cry 'till it gets a date.
Starfish daydream of walks in sand,
Planning vacations, with travel plans unplanned.

Bubbles whisper secrets in a hush,
A clam's relationship: oh what a crush!
Urchins laugh as they twirl about,
Creating a circus that twists the doubt.

In this world where silliness grows,
A dolphin juggles the seaweed and prose.
Forgotten dreams float like lost balloons,
As fishes party beneath the moon.

The laughter echoes, vibrant and bright,
Making shadows dance with delight.
In waters deep where life's a jest,
Every creature strives to be the best.

Glimmers of the Unplumbed

In hidden tides, a treasure gleams,
As fish play poker, plotting wild schemes.
Crabby pirates seek out the best steak,
While mermaids giggle at the choice they make.

Down in the depths, a party ensues,
With bubbles popping like headline news.
A shy anglerfish uses a light,
To attract the laughs on a Saturday night.

An electric eel strikes a pose just right,
While jellyfish glide in a sparkling light.
They spin tales of joy, up and down,
As the ocean laughs in its vibrant gown.

With fishes dressed in frilly attire,
And clam-shells singing, calling for choir.
In the realm where silliness reigns supreme,
Glimmers of laughter shine brighter than a dream.

Where Darkness Meets the Tide

In waters deep where fish do prance,
A squid does tango, what a dance!
A crab in shades of pink and blue,
Says, "Who's got crabs?" Not me, but you!

The seaweed swings, it's quite a sight,
As dolphins giggle, oh so bright.
A whale who sings from deep within,
"Don't take a dive, it's cold and grim!"

The jellyfish, they flit and float,
With tentacles that seem to gloat.
They wave and wink, "Come join the show!"
While anchovies hide, saying, "No, no!"

Yet under waves, a truce is made,
For every fish, a joke displayed.
With laughter bubbling, just one guess,
Be careful, fishy, it's a messy mess!

Beneath the Still Surface

The pond reflects a froggy face,
Croaking jokes at a slower pace.
He jumps and splashes, what a scene,
Chasing bugs like some cuisine!

The turtles boast their ancient lore,
But when they race, they just snore.
Oysters giggle with gleaming shells,
While fish tell tales of ocean smells.

In this still place of squishy sounds,
A catfish pirouettes around.
The bubbles rise, their giggles flow,
As sea cucumbers join the show!

With all this fun beneath the glass,
We find the chorus of the bass.
Lurking deep, the jokes can sting,
With every splash, the laughter rings!

Whispers of the Deep

In murky depths where secrets float,
A salmon writes a funny quote.
The gobies gossip, tails entwined,
While eels make puns that are quite blind.

"Why did the clam refuse to fight?"
"Because he didn't feel quite right!"
The octopus just laughs and says,
"He's probably stuck in hidden bays!"

The bubbles twirl, the sea is grand,
With laughter spilling from the sand.
A sardine slips its little joke,
While underwater, gaggles poke!

With ticklish tides and giggly streams,
The deep's a place of silly dreams.
As laughter echoes far and wide,
What a swim down the giggle tide!

Shadows in the Stillness

In shadows where the fish do hide,
A trout declared, "Let's take a ride!"
The minnows swoosh with cheeky grins,
While bass just roll their fishy fins.

A ghostly crab plays peek-a-boo,
As sea turtles play "stick and glue!"
A flatfish flops, not much to see,
But claims, "I'm under cover, whee!"

The night is filled with fishy cheer,
Where shadows dance without a fear.
They huddle close to share a tale,
"Why don't we swim out and set sail?"

So join the fun beneath the waves,
In sea-edged laughter, the ocean braves.
For every shadow, a joke does lurk,
In stillness found, let joy work!

Waves of Invisible Dread

In the pantry, ghosts do waltz,
Sneaky snacks are their main faults.
Cereal boxes whisper fears,
Crunching loudly, tease the ears.

In the closet, socks do hide,
Missing partners, they confide.
Mismatched foes in colors bright,
Wage a war, all through the night.

Under beds, dust bunnies creep,
Stockpiled secrets, lost in sleep.
When vacuum roars, they scatter fast,
Their fluffy reign, a thing of past.

But the fridge holds the true fright,
Leftovers laughing in the night.
With moldy cheese and spoiling meat,
A comedy of stinky treats.

Secrets That Linger in the Silence

Whispers linger in the air,
Of missing spoons and carousel fare.
The cat's got secrets, I just know,
She rolls her eyes, puts on a show.

Old socks hidden in the wall,
Are they secrets or just a haul?
They camp out there, the bold enlist,
Hiding from the clothes we missed.

In my coffee, dreams may float,
Stirred by spells of hidden quotes.
Sips unravel tales of dread,
Funny how the coffee spread.

When the microwave hums its tune,
I swear it's plotting with the moon.
Popcorn pops with a sly little grin,
Promising chaos, let the fun begin!

Forgotten Realms of the Heart

There's a kingdom beneath my socks,
Rulers made of old lunch boxes.
Beneath the layers of laundry deep,
Lies treasure maps I cannot keep.

In the depths of my old backpack,
Lives a sandwich that's gone off track.
Peanut butter with a twist of fate,
It guards the lore of my lunch plate.

Old teddy bears gather dust,
Negotiate with goldfish just.
A trading pact for a lollipop,
Pillow fights the only way to stop.

Heartfelt secrets in the attic,
Formed of giggles, soft and sporadic.
When I open that chest of fright,
Joy spills out, a silly delight.

The Plunge into Inner Darkness

Time to dive into the drawers,
Where unmatched socks hold secret wars.
Tangled tales of lint and threads,
A world where fashion quietly dreads.

My fridge is a labyrinth of sorts,
Hiding mysteries like past cohorts.
A moldy sandwich smiles wide,
Whispers of a lunch untried.

Pots and pans speak of their uses,
While old spoons gossip, no excuses.
Forks are sworn to silence tight,
As spatulas mingle in the night.

The toilet's tale is quite absurd,
With echoes of all things unheard.
Splashing secrets with every flush,
An inner world that makes me blush.

Murky Waters of the Soul

In a pool where shadows play,
My socks begin to float away.
With each splash, a fish does grin,
Saying, "Sir, you simply can't swim!"

Thoughts swirl round like a bottomless drink,
Mixing flavors without a link.
I ponder deep in muddled glee,
Is that my brain or just a pea?

I dive in with a hopeful cheer,
But all I find is yesterday's beer.
A rubber duck begins to snicker,
"Did you forget? Your jokes are quicker!"

At the depths, a seaweed dance,
To the rhythm of my hapless prance.
Life's just a joke, so laugh with me,
In these waters dark and free!

The Void Cries Softly

In a space where silence hums,
I hear the echoes of my thumbs.
A floating sock that lost its way,
Whispers secrets, or just cliché?

I phone my fears, but they're on mute,
My worries wear a fancy suit.
In this void of thoughts so light,
I wrestle shadows, what a sight!

The loneliness brings out the laughs,
As I trip over my own path.
A whisper says, 'You're not alone!'
'Just keep it down, I need my tone!'

Softly here, the void insists,
"Your humor's grand, you silly mist!"
So I play games with echoes vast,
In this wacky void, I'm unsurpassed!

Beneath Reflections

I stare at mirrors from the past,
Where my fashion sense was quite a blast.
Pants so tight, I can't believe,
That shirt—I still cannot retrieve!

Reflections laugh with misfit glee,
"Beneath this glare, what do you see?"
A glimpse of future, or a fright?
It's hard to tell; my hair's too bright.

A little fish waves with a pout,
Saying, "Hey, why's there water spout?"
Let's dive deep in this wacky trance,
And twirl around in style's dance!

At depths of odd and funny sights,
I swing with glee on swaying nights.
My mind's a funhouse, twist and turn,
In waters shallow, there's much to learn!

Dread Grows

A tiny thought drops like a stone,
Causing ripples in my mind zone.
It bubbles up with mischief's glee,
Shouting loud, "Hey, look at me!"

The more it stirs, the louder it gets,
Filling my head with silly threats.
The fridge says "Check for tasty cheese!"
But I only hear my worries tease!

I step outside, it seems to sneak,
Wearing a hat, dancing unique.
"Don't be scared!" it giggles bold,
"I only bite when I'm not told!"

So dread becomes a jolly joke,
Like a prancing, playful bloke.
In the chaos of my mind's parade,
I laugh with dread, a friend well made!

Entrapments of the Hidden

In corners dark, I've trapped my thoughts,
Like laundry piles and rusty pots.
Dust bunnies dance, oh what a sight,
Laughing at fears while taking flight!

What lies beneath is purely hilarious,
Like an old cat who thinks it's serious.
Hidden pranks and chuckles spring,
As my worries just laugh and fling!

A sock puppet rises from the floor,
"Hey there, buddy! Don't ignore!"
Laughter erupts from shadows near,
As they plot to tickle my fear!

So let the hidden play their game,
In closets where we hide our shame.
With a wink and giggle, there's no bluff,
In these traps, humor's always enough!

Echoes from the Dark

In the depths where whispers creep,
Fish wear hats and dance with glee,
A sardine sings a tune so steep,
While crabs play cards, quite fancy-free.

Bubbles rise, like giggles shared,
Octopuses cracking jokes so sly,
A coral choir, all well-prepared,
For coral-reffed tunes that make you cry.

Eels in ties, they strut along,
With seaweed wigs, all decked in style,
They form a band, play notes so wrong,
But fish will listen for a while.

So here in this odd, wet retreat,
Where laughter echoes, oh so loud,
The tuneful tales, though bittersweet,
In waves of humor, we're all proud.

Beneath the Layers of Time

In pockets deep where sunbeams fade,
A clam's got secrets, slathered in sand,
It flips through pages of old mermaid trade,
Selling seashells at the undersea stand.

The barnacles gossip, oh what a sight,
While starfish lounge in a five-o'clock chair,
They sip on seaweed, feeling just right,
Making plans for a fishy fair.

Time rolls like waves, with a splattering sound,
Turtles boast of ancient galas,
Where jellyfish waltz in a whirlwind round,
And seahorses win in their silk-suit pajamas.

So dive in deep, where laughter is found,
In currents of joy, we twirl and we spin,
With every tick-tock from the ocean's surround,
Life's just a shell, with a giggle within.

Secrets of the Silent Depths

In the hush of deep, there's a tickle or two,
Where fish tell secrets with winks and a nod,
They've plotted a quest, for a treasure quite blue,
With a map drawn by squid, it seems a bit flawed.

Anemones giggle as they jazzily sway,
While gobies play dress-up, in outfits so bold,
With bits of old pearls, they steal the display,
As the anglerfish grins, all glittering gold.

The sea cucumbers ponder what's next,
In their slow-motion race, they take it all in,
While flatfish just flat-out seem perplexed,
As they laugh at the jokes from an old sea sponge's grin.

So, come explore where the fun never ends,
In a world full of quirks, we'll cherish the jest,
With each joyful tale, the weirdness transcends,
In the silent depths, laughter is best.

Veins of the Forgotten Sea

Through watery veins, where silliness flows,
A walrus recites poetry in rhyme,
With laughter and snorts, and flippers that pose,
He jokes with the seals, oh what a good time!

The treasure chest rusts, but the humor is bright,
With octopuses' arms playing tag in the tide,
As conchs tell tall tales in the pale moonlight,
Fish gather 'round for a spin on the slide.

A crab with a monocle ponders his fate,
While mermaids slip by on their glittery skates,
The dolphin dons shades, looking really quite great,
In a splish-splash soirée at the oceanic gates.

So dive into laughs in this current parade,
With silliness swimming at every twist bend,
In veins of the sea, where the jokes never fade,
Join the merriment, my friend, don't pretend!